Ride a Winner!

Karen Bush

Illustrated by Maggie Raynor

First published in Great Britain in 2002 by
The Pony Club
NAC Stoneleigh Park
Kenilworth
Warwickshire
CV8 2RW

2 4 6 8 10 9 7 5 3 1

Copyright © 2002 Karen Bush

Illustrations © 2002 Maggie Raynor

ISBN 0-9541531-2-X

Edited and designed by Paul Harding

Printed in Great Britain by Biddles Limited

Introduction

Go to any horse show and you'll find that the competition can be pretty fierce at even the lowest of levels. Obviously, it helps if you have a good horse, some talent as a rider and plenty of determination, but these qualities on their own aren't enough if you want to enjoy any degree of success. To maximise the potential of both you and your horse, you also have to be prepared to adopt a professional approach. This involves planning ahead and preparing yourself as thoroughly as possible during the weeks before a show, developing an eye for detail and, on the day, ensuring that you do all the right things in the classes you have entered.

Whether you are just starting out competing or an old hand at it, you'll find plenty of useful advice in this book. Do remember, though, that whilst being placed up in the 'ribbons' is nice, competing isn't just about winning. It's also about increasing your knowledge and developing your skills out of the ring and, most importantly of all, enjoying yourself and having a fun day out too.

Contents

Contents

Choosing your classes

You will find advertisements for shows in local newspapers and horsy magazines. Ask at feed merchants, riding schools, livery yards and saddlery shops too - they may have a schedule you can take with you. If not, make a note of the address to write to for one.

- When requesting schedules from show secretaries, don't forget to include a stamped, self-addressed envelope.
- Even if you don't own a horse, you can still compete. Many riding schools run both open and client-only shows for which you can hire a horse (provided you are a regular customer).
- Make sure you fill in entry forms correctly and clearly.
- Remember to enclose payment when you send off your entries.
- Post your entry form off in plenty of time before the closing date. If it arrives late, it may not be accepted.
- You can wait and enter on the day if you prefer, but if the class is full you may not get a place. Not only is this disappointing if you have worked hard in preparation, late entries often cost more too.
- Some classes, like dressage and cross-country events (where starting times need to be worked out in advance) are pre-entry only.
- Check to see if you will need any papers - for membership, registration, vaccination, etc. - and that they have been kept up to date and will still be valid on the day of the show.
- If the schedule states that you have to telephone for a starting time, make a note of the number, day and time you should call. Failure to call could result in being eliminated from the competition.
- Remember to keep the schedule after you've sent off your entry form, as you may need it to remind you of the classes you've entered and how to get to the showground.

Making your entries

When a show schedule arrives, read through it carefully and use a pencil to highlight the classes you're interested in. Then you can start to narrow down your choices.

- Be selective and don't be tempted to enter as many classes as possible in the hope that you'll win something in one of them. You will just end up over-tiring yourself and your horse, and won't do yourself justice at all.

- Make sure that you meet all the conditions stated in the schedule with regard to horse and rider age and winnings. If showing, your horse should also be the right type for the class.

- Pick classes that are well within your ability and that of your horse. It's best to compete at a slightly lower level than you work at when schooling at home to ensure neither of you struggle to cope with the demands of the class. You don't want to lose confidence and become disheartened, let alone run the risk of injury.

- If you want to enter two classes that will be running at the same time, don't enter both but pick the one you feel you will do best at. If you have to keep flitting from one ring to another, you will be hurried, flustered and unable to give your best effort in either.

- Don't enter more than two showjumping classes or you will over-tire your horse.

- If you have a young or new horse with little or unknown show experience, choose one or two quiet and simple classes for your first outing together.

- Check that your horse's insurance covers him for the type of competition you are planning to enter.

- Choose classes that you and your horse will enjoy. If you are both enthusiastic about it, you're much more likely to do well!

Novelty classes

In addition to the more conventional showing and jumping classes, you will often find that local unaffiliated shows run a few 'novelty' classes. Although these may contain elements of showing or jumping, they don't fit entirely into either of these categories but can be great fun to participate in. If your horse has only limited jumping ability or his conformation isn't quite good enough for showing, these may suit him much better, and will give you the chance to compete on level terms with other riders. Some of the classes advertised in schedules include:

- Horse and Hound: This involves horse and rider jumping round a low course of fences, at the end of which dog and handler take over and tackle either the same or a slightly smaller course. Check the rules carefully, as the rider may be required to pass their riding whip over to the dog handler at a specific hand-over point - as in a relay race - before being allowed to start their round. Organisers will often stipulate that the dog must be kept on a lead throughout to avoid it from escaping and running loose across the showground. The fastest clear round is judged to be the winner.

- Family Horse / Pony: This class is judged on manners and suitability as an all-round family ride, so the horse should behave impeccably and be capable of carrying a small adult as well as a child. Sometimes a fence is included, but this will be fairly low and undemanding. The rider may be asked to do something to demonstrate the horse's steadiness and reliability such as dismounting and remounting again whilst it stands quietly.

- Handy Horse / Pony: Horse and rider will be required to negotiate a series of obstacles, such as bending in and out through plastic cones, walking over a sheet of plastic, opening and shutting gates, picking up objects, jumping a small fence, and standing at a given point whilst being dismounted and remounted. Marks may be awarded or deducted for completion of each 'hazard' and the whole round is often timed. A certain amount of rider agility is an asset, whilst the horse needs to be obedient, sensible and steady in temperament.

- Veteran: Generally for equines aged over 15 years, these classes are either in-hand or under saddle. In ridden classes, you may be asked to give a short individual show. Usually judged on condition, well-being and soundness, manners, and to a lesser extent, conformation may also be taken into account.

- Best Turned Out: Also sometimes called 'Tack and Turnout' classes, these are ideal for perfectionists with a good eye for detail. Conformation and performance are not taken into account, but both horse and rider need to be spotlessly clean and wearing the correct clothing and saddlery - either hacking or hunting dress as stated in the schedule.

- Best Rider: Sometimes called 'Equitation' classes, it is the rider's ability to sit well and ride effectively which is important, rather than the horse's conformation. The more obedient and well-schooled your horse is, the more favourably you will be judged. You are likely to be asked to give a brief individual show, and sometimes competitors are asked to change horses with each other in order to demonstrate their knowledge and skill when riding an unknown animal.

- Fancy Dress: You don't need to spend a lot of money on an outfit: ingenuity and originality usually count more. Make sure you try out your costume at home first to ensure that your horse is not alarmed by anything that you - or he - will be wearing.

Countdown to the show

A little forward planning is needed for you and your horse to be ready for the first show of the season. Make a list of all the things you will need to do during the weeks leading up to it, working backwards from the competition date.

<u>6 weeks to go</u>

- Work out a programme to get your horse into shape and fit enough to cope with the type of classes you intend to enter.
- Start looking out for and sending off for show schedules. Don't be tempted to attend as many shows as possible, as your horse could become stale.
- If you need advice on feeding your horse, contact the feed company whose products you use. Many manufacturers have free telephone helplines you can contact or websites you can go to.
- Get yourself into shape too! Perhaps you need to get a little fitter or to start having regular lessons to help improve your riding skills.
- Make a wall-planner to help you keep track of show dates and other important information.

<u>5 weeks to go</u>

- Check that you know the rules for those classes you intend entering. Send off to governing bodies for rule books you need.
- Practise loading your horse into a trailer or horsebox to ensure he is happy and relaxed about it, and not likely to be difficult on the big day.

<u>4 weeks to go</u>

- Start to spend more time on grooming.
- Introduce regular schooling sessions.
- If you do not own your own vehicle, make travelling arrangements. It may seem a bit early, but it's best to arrange trailer or horsebox hire well in advance to ensure you get a booking

Countdown to the show

3 weeks to go
- Check that all your saddlery fits your horse, and get repairs done.
- If you will be using different saddlery or bits to normal, practise riding using them so both you and your horse have time to become accustomed to them.

2 weeks to go
- Look out all your own competition clothes and make sure you have everything you will need: get your jacket dry cleaned, if necessary.
- If you are going to need help on the day, arrange now for somebody to be your assistant.
- Start doing any mane and tail pulling necessary.
- If you are doing a dressage class, learn your test and practice riding through each of the movements.
- If you are showing, work out an individual show.

1 week to go
- Inspect your horse's shoes and have him reshod if needed. Don't forget to ask for stud holes if you're planning to use studs.
- Trim up jawlines and legs if appropriate.
- Double-check the date, location and time of the show.
- If you are required to ring for starting times, remember to telephone the organisers on the day and at the time specified on the schedule.
- Buy any additional plaiting equipment or hoof and coat care products you will need.
- To help put a final polish on your performance, book a last lesson with your horse.
- Get out any documentation you will need to produce at the show and check it again.

Learning the rules

It is important to be familiar with the rules for the classes you want to compete in. Unaffiliated shows tend to follow the same rules as affiliated ones so even if you are competing at a more modest level, contact the governing body of that particular discipline to obtain a copy of them. Pony Club and Riding Club competitions may differ slightly, so if you plan to enter a show run by either of them, make sure you find out any variations in advance.

- Once you have your copy of the rule book, take the time to read it thoroughly.
- Go to a few shows as a spectator and watch what goes on in the arena. You will learn a lot and have a clearer idea of what is expected of you when it is your turn to have a go.
- Many competitors will be only too happy to answer any questions you may have, but choose your moment. Just when someone is about to go in the ring or is busy getting ready is not a good time.
- Volunteer to assist a friend at a competition they are entering.
- Have some lessons from an instructor who has first hand experience or knowledge of the classes you want to enter. As well as practical help with preparing yourself and your horse, they will be able to explain exactly what you will need to do in the ring and also, if you aren't sure, give advice on the classes most suitable for you.
- Offer to help out at a local show for the day. Lending a hand to build showjumping courses, act as a dressage judge's writer, be a jump judge, or help as a ring steward or in another capacity, is a good way of increasing your knowledge. If you tend to suffer from pre-show nerves, competing will be far less terrifying if you know what goes on behind the scenes.

Keeping track of things

As well as hard work, success relies on good organisation and a certain amount of paperwork - not just filling in entry forms. A wall-planner will not only help you to keep track of show dates, but also allow you to see at a glance what things need to be done in preparation, so you don't forget or leave anything until the very last minute. You can buy one or make your own, using a large sheet of paper, card or the back of a piece of wallpaper. Stick it on the wall where you will be able to see and write on it easily.

- Write on it all the show dates you plan to attend. Then, enter dates for vaccinations, teeth rasping, shoeing and worming so they are kept up to date and you can be sure they don't clash with competition days. If you miss a vaccination date - even if it is only by a day - you will have to repeat the whole course all over again, and some show rules insist that you won't be allowed to compete until you can prove that your horse is fully protected.

- Use your wall-planner to remind you when you have to drop off or pick up saddlery repairs. It can also help you remember when you have to ring for starting times, have a lesson booked, and the closing dates for entries.

- Next to your wall-planner, pin up a copy of your fitness programme.

- Hang up a jotter pad and pencil too, or a wipe clean notice board, to make quick notes on.

- Buy or make a special folder to keep all your horse's documentation in - such as insurance papers, vaccination certificates, and registration papers - so that everything is together in one place and easy to find when you need it.

- Keep a second folder for schedules and entry forms.

Checklists

If you get to the showground only to find you've left some vital piece of equipment at home, you probably won't be able to go back to fetch it and still be in time for your class. Write out a checklist at least a week in advance of your first show, itemising everything you can think of which you'll need. This will give you time to add on anything else that you subsequently remember over the next few days. Once your list is complete, write or type it out neatly on a clean sheet of paper. Use one side for your horse, and the other for your own things.

- Get the list laminated at a stationers or place it inside a clear plastic sleeve. This will protect it from damage, and you can tick off each item as you get it ready using a felt tip pen. Later on, you can wipe off the ink with a damp cloth and use the checklist again next time.

- Old plastic tubs with close fitting lids (from products like ice cream or margarine) make handy containers for hair grips, studs and other odds and ends. They're far less likely to get lost or mislaid than a handful of small, loose things. Label each container clearly so you can quickly see what is in them.

- Make sure that any liquids like hoof oils or coat gloss have leak-proof lids and, for additional safety, place them in separate containers in case of spillages.

- Use your checklist again when it is time to pack up to return home, so you do not leave anything behind at the showground.

- The checklists on the opposite page give you an idea of the sort of things you might include - add anything extra you will need or delete things you won't.

Checklists

Horse

- ☐ Grooming kit
- ☐ Damp sponges in plastic bags
- ☐ Towel
- ☐ Scissors
- ☐ Plaiting kit
- ☐ Travelling first aid kit
- ☐ Headcollar and leadrope
- ☐ Saddle
- ☐ Girth
- ☐ Bridle
- ☐ Spare pair of reins
- ☐ Spare pair of stirrup leathers
- ☐ Water bucket
- ☐ Container of water
- ☐ Small haynet
- ☐ Travelling clothes
- ☐ Tack cleaning kit
- ☐ Boots and bandages
- ☐ Fly repellent
- ☐ Skep, rubber gloves/shovel
- ☐ Cooler
- ☐ Rainsheet
- ☐ String to tie up with
- ☐ Lungeing kit if needed

Rider

- ☐ First aid kit
- ☐ Riding clothes
- ☐ Clothes brush
- ☐ Boot polish and brushes
- ☐ Riding hat
- ☐ Hairnet, grips, ribbons
- ☐ Whip/show cane
- ☐ Buttonhole
- ☐ Spurs
- ☐ Schedule
- ☐ Map
- ☐ Money
- ☐ Lunch
- ☐ Paperwork
- ☐ Notebook and pen
- ☐ Watch

Horse fitness

Your horse needs to be fit enough to take part in the classes you wish to enter without becoming unduly stressed. An unfit horse not only stands less chance of success in competition if he becomes fatigued, but also runs the risk of injury. He will tend to sweat more profusely (losing fluids rapidly) and may become severely dehydrated, which could have serious - even life-threatening - consequences.

- Different disciplines make different demands on your horse. Devise a programme to help him achieve the appropriate level of fitness for the type of competition you wish to enter; ask your instructor for help if you are unsure.
- Keep an eye out for any signs of galling occurring in the girth region. Run a hand down all four legs before and after exercise to spot any signs of heat or swelling which could indicate strain from doing too much work too soon.
- When hacking out, send your horse positively forward into the bridle so that he is using himself properly.
- Try to find routes you can take that include hills when out on hacks.
- Adjust your horse's diet as his fitness programme progresses, but always remember to increase the amount of exercise you are giving before you begin to increase the quantity of feed.
- No matter what discipline you are taking part in, incorporate some schooling as well as hacking work into your fitness programme to improve general balance, suppleness and obedience.
- As your horse becomes fitter you will notice that his shape starts to change. Check that your saddle still fits correctly, and get any necessary alterations made so it doesn't pinch or cause soreness.

Rider fitness

It's no good getting your horse fit if you aren't going to be up to the challenge of competing as well. If you get tired, it will interfere with your ability to ride well because you will start to lose the ability to give clear aids or to assist the horse when necessary. Just as seriously, rider fatigue leads to loss of good posture, so can cause the horse to become unbalanced, distracted and to tire more quickly himself.

- Increase the amount of exercise you take. Instead of travelling by car or bus, try to walk at least part of the way.

- When walking anywhere, step up the pace a bit and instead of strolling, really stride out briskly.

- Swimming, jogging, cycling and skipping regularly are also good ways to get yourself into better physical shape.

- Take the stairs instead of using the lift. Once you can cope comfortably with walking up them, try running.

- Ask your riding instructor to show you some stretching exercises you can do whilst dismounted. As well as increasing your general flexibility, they can be a useful way of warming up before riding.

- If you aren't very good at sticking to a personal fitness programme, team up with a friend or member of your family. You'll help to keep each other motivated.

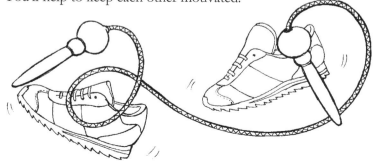

Coat and hoof care

Getting your horse looking his very best for a show is as much about good stable management as it is last minute polishing up.

- If your horse's feet are to be kept healthy and in good shape, they should be shod regularly and receive attention from the farrier every four to six weeks.

- If you have a show date close to when the farrier is due, check the condition of the shoes in case they're becoming loose or worn.

- Good hoof and coat growth and condition are a sign of inner health. If the coat tends to look dry and dull, and the feet prone to brittleness and cracking, ask your vet to check over your horse in case there are any physical problems.

- Suitable feeding is also essential to create healthy feet and a lustrous coat. Contact an equine nutritionist if you need help in devising an appropriate diet.

- Coat bloom can be given a helping hand by adding soya oil, linseed oil or linseed jelly to your horse's feed. If you are already using a show or conditioning diet, this probably won't be necessary as these feeds often already contain high levels of oil. (Check with the manufacturer if you aren't sure).

- Regular grooming and strapping with a pad or wisp will have a beneficial massaging effect for both the coat and muscles as it stimulates the circulation. It will also help to remove excess grease and spread the natural coat oils.

- If you use coat gloss products, don't apply them beneath the saddle area as they may cause it to slip.

- Correct schooling is vital in developing top line and muscle definition.

Bathing

If the weather is warm enough, you may want to bath your horse to help remove grease and grass or stable stains from his coat. This is best done two or three days before the show because it will also remove the natural oils from his coat which help to make it shine. However, if you own a grey or white horse, or one which normally lives out, you may not have much choice but to do it the day before the show.

- Put a nylon web headcollar on your horse while bathing him rather than leather. Make sure it is clean, or else dirty marks will be left on his head.
- Use warm water rather than cold, as it will penetrate the coat better, be less chilling for your horse, and work up a better lather.
- Wash and gently towel dry the head first of all, taking care not to get soapy suds in his eyes. Once this is done you can get on with the rest of his body without worrying about him standing around getting chilled while you do the more fiddly bits.
- Wet the coat all over, then use a shampoo specifically formulated for horses. Don't apply it directly to the coat, but to either the water or a wet sponge, as directed on the shampoo packaging.
- In circular movements, work the shampoo well into the coat using a rubber curry comb. This will help bring all the dirt right up from the roots of the hairs.
- Once you've finished the coat, wet and shampoo the mane and tail.
- Rinse off thoroughly - make sure all traces of shampoo are removed or it will leave the coat looking dull and scurfy, and make your horse feel itchy.
- Use a sweat scraper to remove surplus water from the coat, then walk your horse in hand until dry. Put a rug with a wicking action on him if the weather is on the cool side.

Mane and tail care

Don't neglect manes and tails: if they are carefully maintained, they will enhance your horse's appearance and be easier to plait neatly.

- If the mane or tail needs to be pulled, do it gradually over a period of time. If you try to do too much at once it will make your horse sore and inclined to rub, breaking the hairs off short.

- Hairs are easier to remove after exercise when your horse is still warm.

- Taking just a few hairs at a time from the underside, pull the mane so that it is the thickness you require, and then pull to reduce length.

- Use an old clipper blade to shorten the mane if it is already fairly fine but too long, and you don't wish to make it any thinner.

- If your horse really objects to having his mane pulled, use a thinning comb instead.

- To be the right length to plait, the mane will need to be shortened to around 15 - 20 cm (6" - 8").

- When pulling a tail, do a little at a time - stepping back to assess the effect after every few pulls - as it can be very easy to overdo things and end up with unsightly bald patches.

- Don't do any pulling if your horse is one of those breeds which should be shown in a 'natural' state. (This means having a full, flowing mane and tail).

- Dampening the tail and putting a tail bandage on will help to encourage the hairs to lie flat. Never leave it on for more than a few hours, and only while your horse is stabled.

- You will find it easier to put on a tail bandage if you first drape the tail over one of your shoulders.

- When removing a tail bandage, undo the tapes and slide it straight down the tail. If you twist it, the hairs will be skewed to the side.

Mane and tail care

- On a day to day basis, use your fingers to tidy the long tail hairs and remove any bedding from them. Gently tease out any tangles.

- When you do brush out the tail properly, use only the softest of brushes so you don't break the hairs and leave the tail looking wispy and thin. Spraying on a little mane and tail conditioner or detangler will help the brush to slide through more easily.

- A sparse tail can be given more body by washing and then plaiting it from the bottom of the dock to the end whilst still damp, securing with a rubber band. When dry and unplaited again, it will have a slightly wavy, thicker appearance.

- A white tail can often develop a yellowish appearance. Wash it using one of the proprietary tail whitening products available from good saddlers, although if it has become heavily stained, you may need to do this several times during the weeks before the show to get it looking really good.

- Don't use mane or tail conditioners and detanglers before plaiting, or the hairs will be far too slippery to grasp firmly. Only apply them to long tail hairs after you have finished plaiting at the top.

- If the mane has a tendency to stand up or change direction in the way it lies along the neck, train it to lie all on one side by putting in loose stable plaits for a few hours. Never leave them in if your horse is likely to rub them when left unsupervised.

Plaiting

Anyone can learn to plait, and with a bit of practice you can become really expert at it. Plaits should always be sewn in if you are showing, using thread of the same colour as the mane. For jumping and dressage classes, elastic bands are fine if you prefer to use them, and are quicker to use.

- A plaiting apron is handy. Buy one or make your own by adding pockets to a normal apron to keep scissors, combs, elastic bands and thread in, and give it a reinforced fabric section on the bib part to push your needle into.

- A dressmaker's needle-threader is very cheap to buy and makes threading needles much easier and quicker.

- Stand on a sturdy box to give yourself a bit of height. If you have to keep reaching upwards your arms will quickly grow tired, and your plaits won't look so neat.

- Dampen each section of mane before plaiting it, or use a little setting gel to make the hairs more manageable and to prevent any wispy bits from sticking out. Be careful not to get any gel on your horse's neck.

- Keep plaits tight as you work.

- Choose the number of plaits to best suit your horse. A long neck will look longer with lots of little plaits, whilst a short one will look even more so with too few, big plaits.

- If the neck is fairly heavy, place your plaits close beneath the line of the crest. If it is a little weak and lacking in muscle, place them along the top.

- If the mane is plaited, the tail should also be either plaited or pulled, rather than left full.

- Plait at least two thirds of the way down the dock: a little further if the tailbone is a bit short.

Plaiting

- Take care when removing tail a bandage from a plaited tail - unwind it carefully rather than pulling it off.
- If your horse needs to have his mane left long for showing classes you can still create a smart appearance for dressage competitions by doing a long running plait.
- If you are fairly confident that your plaits will stay in place and know your horse won't rub them, you can plait the mane the night before a show to save time in the morning. Leave forelocks and tails until the day itself.
- Keep hay or bedding from sticking to finished plaits by placing a stocking leg over them, held in place by an elastic band over the top of each plait.
- Use a dressmaker's stitch unpicker to undo sewn plaits. It's quicker than using scissors, and you won't accidentally cut through the hairs.

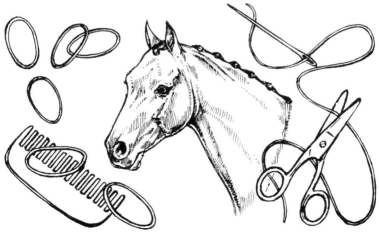

Trimming up

A little judicious trimming can do a lot to smarten up your horse's appearance. If you will be showing him, check the guidelines laid down by governing bodies to find out what is correct for his type and breed. Generally, those horses which are shown in a 'natural' state should not be trimmed at all, although a minimal amount of tidying up may be permissible in some instances.

- Ask someone to slide an arm beneath the dock so that the tail is raised to the same height it will be carried at when working. Run your hand down the length of the tail, holding the hairs together in a tight bunch and cut the end square at around 15 - 20 cm (6" - 8") below the point of hock. If the tail is very thick, using clippers instead of scissors will prevent the end from looking stepped.

- Use a comb to make two straight partings and cut out a small section of mane to create a bridle path, so the headpiece sits better. Remove only as wide a strip of mane as necessary, and check before cutting that it is in the right place.

- Use scissors or run clippers along the lower jawline.

- A plastic safety razor quickly and neatly removes long muzzle hairs.

- Fold the sides of the ears together and use scissors to trim along the edges. Never cut hairs growing inside the ears.

- Trimming the legs with scissors and a comb takes time, but will produce a neat, more natural looking effect than clipping. Comb upwards against the lie of the hairs, and snip off all those which stick through between the teeth.

- If your horse has a hogged mane but a slightly weak neck, clip it a week or so before the show so it grows just enough to give the impression of more bulk.

t isn't essential to use studs in your horse's shoes, but if the going isn't
leal, they'll give him better grip and more confidence in the ground .

Keep stud holes free of mud and grit with metal sleepers, plastic
stud plugs, or by packing them with a small wad of cotton wool
soaked in a little oil, twisted in to ensure a firm fit.

If you use cotton wool, ask your farrier for a couple of spare
horseshoe nails to pick it out with.

Keep all your studs, tap and spanner together in a small box to
ensure you don't lose anything.

When buying new studs, check that their thread size matches that
of the stud holes.

Do not transport your horse with studs in. Put them in just before
you require them, and remove them again immediately afterwards.

There are lots of different shapes and sizes of studs to choose
from. Generally speaking, use small, sharp studs when the going
is firm, and broader, blunt ones when it is soft.

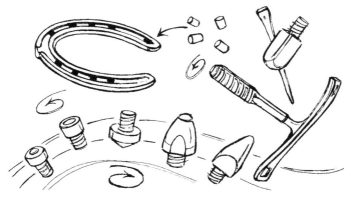

Rider dress

Check that you have suitable clothes for the class you are competing in, and in case you need to make a special order for something new you will need, go shopping in plenty of time.

- If you haven't worn your show clothes for some time, try them all on to check that they still fit.
- Check rule books to see if there are any specific items of clothing which it is compulsory to wear for a particular class or phase of competition - such as a back protector, gloves or a jockey skull cap.
- Look at the labels on your hard hat and back protector to ensure they conform to the most recent safety guidelines.
- As well as being appropriate for your class, your clothes should also be clean and worn correctly so that your appearance is neat and professional.
- Do not wear jewellery.
- If you want to wear make up, keep it light and as natural as possible.
- Hair should be tidy and secure. If you will be wearing a hairnet use a fine mesh one which is the same colour as your hair. Longer hair can either be plaited or worn in a bun. Use a bun ring if it isn't quite long enough for a really smart effect.
- Don't wear badges unless they are required for your class.
- Practice riding in your show clothes at least a couple of times so that you feel relaxed and comfortable in them, and can check that you are able to move freely.
- If you wear a buttonhole, it should be small and discreet - not the size of a floral tribute!
- Trim the edges of show numbers with a pair of scissors, rounding off the corners to make them look neater, and less likely to curl up.

Always check that the saddlery you intend to use is permitted. Read the rule book or ask an experienced person if you are uncertain.

Inspect all your saddlery for areas of wear or weak stitching, and check that bits, stirrup irons and other metal items are neither worn nor distorted.

All your saddlery should be clean, particularly if you are taking part in a showing class. Maintain and nourish it on a regular basis, because no amount of last-minute polishing can disguise the fact that leather saddlery has been neglected in the past. It will also help to extend its life and make it safer to use.

Adding a little washing-up liquid to hot water will help remove grease when cleaning saddlery.

In classes where the judge might ride your horse, there must be enough adjustment possible in stirrup leathers to accommodate riders who may be taller or shorter than you.

Use a dead match stick to remove soap from buckle holes.

Liquid glycerine soaps or leather wipes are useful for last minute touch-ups just before going in the ring, as they give a nice sheen, smear less than hard soaps and won't clog up holes.

Delicate bridlework is fine in the showring, but for showjumping or riding cross-country it should be more robust.

Flatwork

As part of your preparations, schooling your horse on the flat is just as important for jumping or showing classes as it is for dressage competitions. It will help make your horse more supple and obedient, as well as helping to build muscle in the right places.

- Develop your ability to ride precisely and use space efficiently by marking out a 20 x 40 metre area to work in, using letter markers set out at the appropriate distances. You can either buy these, or make your own by painting the letters on a set of plastic traffic cones, or on the sides of plastic 'Bloks'.

- If you work in a field used for grazing, put all your schooling equipment away after you have finished so that it does not become damaged or cause injury. Never ride in the field if loose animals are grazing in it.

- If your horse tends to be spooky about dressage boards, place jump poles or halved plastic drainpipe covers along the edges of the schooling area to help accustom him to them.

- Choose an area of ground to work on which is fairly level and well drained. Don't ride next to low or barbed wire fencing, or where you will need to pass beneath low, overhanging tree branches. Trim back any tussocky areas of grass.

- Give your horse time to work in at the walk before starting trot or canter work. This allows the muscles to warm up gradually, and reduces the risk of strains occurring.

- Try to be imaginative in your schooling to keep the work varied and interesting for your horse.

- Have regular lessons on your horse. This will ensure you are working along the right lines, and provides you with plenty of new ideas for exercises you can try when schooling on your own.

Flatwork

- Use traffic cones to mark out different sizes of circles and other movements to help increase the accuracy of your figure riding.

- Try schooling occasionally with some music playing in the background. You can buy audio tapes with music specifically recorded for riding to: ask your instructor to suggest some appropriate selections. As well as being a good way of improving the rhythm of your horse's gaits, you will find it can have a positive effect on your riding.

- Look out some soothing classical music to listen to before a competition as well: if you tend to get nervous, it can be very effective in calming and relaxing you.

- Don't forget that you can still do schooling work when you're out hacking. Practise shortening and lengthening stride, and asking for upwards and downwards transitions. When off the road, you can also practice things like lateral work and canter leads.

- Reward your horse with a pat and a word of praise when he makes a good effort at doing something. Allow him to stretch and relax on a long rein in walk for a minute or two before starting again.

- Work equally on all three gaits, and on both reins.

- As well as concentrating on how your horse is moving, be aware of your own position, and try to improve it at the same time. The better you sit, the clearer and more effective your aids will be, and the easier it is for your horse to respond to your requests.

- Don't overdo things and work your horse to the point where one or both of you feel exhausted.

- Always try and finish on a good note. It's better to finish a little earlier if things have gone well and your horse has tried hard, than to continue just for the sake of it.

Preparing for showing classes

In addition to being able to turn your horse out immaculately, you chances of success in the show ring will be improved by paying attention to detail and schooling on the flat (and over fences if the class involves jumping).

- Accustom your horse to working in the company of others by getting together with friends, joining a group lesson at a riding school, or attending instructional mounted days run by your Pony or Riding Club.
- To ensure your horse will leave the line when asked, practise standing him in line with a few others and riding out away from it
- Teach basic manners so your horse will stand still, remain motionless when mounted or dismounted, and only walk of when told to.
- Make sure your horse is used to being mounted both from the ground and from a leg-up.
- Spend time teaching him to lead out freely in hand in walk and trot
- If entering a class where the judge will ride him, get your horse used to being ridden by other people. This will also give you the opportunity to see what weak areas of schooling need to be worked on.

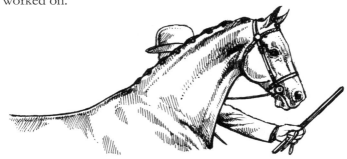

Planning an individual show

During most showing classes you will be asked to give an individual show. Work out what you are going to do and practise it a few times at home to ensure that it will look easy, fluent and professional on the day.

- Whilst waiting in the line up for your turn, look at the area you have to work in and decide how best to fit your individual show into the space available.

- As the competitor before you is riding their show, make sure your horse is standing alertly so he is ready to move forward briskly when asked.

- When called out of line, walk forward a few strides and halt so the judge can take a closer look at him before you begin your individual show.

- Keep your show short, sweet and simple. It should last between one and three minutes, and include walk, trot and canter on both reins, a halt and if appropriate for the class, gallop.

- Aim to show off your horse's best points. If he has a really good trot, show more of this and less of his worst gait.

- Don't be over-ambitious and attempt to do anything which you cannot be absolutely sure will be successful.

- Except when you return to your original position after finishing your show, try to avoid riding behind the line up, as the judge won't be able to see you properly.

- A figure of eight can look extremely effective, but only if ridden really well. Otherwise it can highlight any stiffness, resistance and lack of balance. If you want to incorporate this movement into your show, mark it out with cones at home to improve your accuracy, and practice until you can execute it faultlessly.

Learning a dressage test

When you first get your copy of the dressage test you will be riding read through the sheet carefully to ensure you understand all of the movements so that you will ride them correctly in your class.

- Some people find it easier to learn a test if there is some kind of visual reference. It is possible to buy test sheets which have a diagram of each movement accompanying the text. Alternatively you can draw out each of the movements yourself on a separate piece of paper.
- If you are riding more than one test, learn one thoroughly first before starting on the next. It's much easier than attempting to memorise both at the same time.
- Draw a plan of the arena on a piece of paper. Running through the test using a finger or tip of a pen will help you to learn it.
- At home, mark out a scaled down version of a dressage arena using bean poles. By running round it on foot, you can practice your test without a horse.
- Ride through the whole test a couple of times to get a feel for how it flows, but not to the point where your horse knows it better than you do. This may cause him to anticipate the next movement and lead to a loss of accuracy which you will lose marks for.
- If you want to concentrate on improving individual movements, ride them out of order, but finish each by joining them onto another. This will develop your ability to link them together rather than constantly stopping and starting.
- Practise riding your test and schooling in an arena of the appropriate dimensions. Define the edges using jump poles or halved plastic drainpipe covers, and buy or make a set of letter markers to place around the outside.

Calling a test

If you are really worried that you might lose your way during a dressage test, ask someone to call it for you. Bear in mind that a caller is just a memory prompt - not an excuse for not learning the test at all - otherwise it will lack fluency.

- Tests can be called in most dressage competitions, but there are exceptions - such as during Horse Trials - so do check first.
- Arrange to have a dress rehearsal with your caller to make sure you can hear them clearly, and to establish how far in advance you want each movement called.
- Although the caller will be reading from a copy of the test, they need to be familiar with the sequence of movements, to be able to identify them being ridden, and to know where each of the arena markers are.
- The caller may only read out each of the movements as they appear on the test sheet. Any other assistance may result in your disqualification.
- It will make the test sheet easier to read at a glance if you enlarge it with a photocopier.
- The caller should stand outside the arena, ideally opposite the E or B marker. In this position they will have a good view of horse and rider throughout the test, and since they will never be much further than 20 metres distance away, it will be easier for you to hear them at all times. Neither will they obscure the judge's view.

Showjumping schooling

If you overdo jumping practice, instead of honing your skills you will cause your horse to become stale and unenthusiastic. Twice a week is generally quite sufficient, perhaps reducing to just once the week before a competition.

- Give your practice fences a fresh coat of paint so that the ones you meet in competition won't alarm your horse.

- Don't jump the same fence again and again. Build different shapes of fences - uprights, ascending and square spreads - to keep them interesting and teach you both how to approach each type.

- Occasionally doing a little gridwork adds variety. It will develop your horse's athletic ability over fences, and also help you to develop an eye for a good stride and learn how to ride through combinations, and related distances.

- School over fences less frequently and over smaller obstacles if the ground is hard (unless you have access to an all weather surface or indoor school).

- Horses tend to jump more confidently at home, so try and practice in other locations too. Take it in turns with friends to jump at each other's yards, or hire local facilities.

- Don't neglect improving your course riding skills too, as it is vital to learn to ride an accurate line between fences.

Cross-country schooling

Good flatwork is as essential for successful and safe cross-country riding as it is for jumping ability, so don't neglect this aspect of your horse's education even if you are only planning to do Hunter Trials rather than eventing. Your horse will be more supple and obedient, better able to realise his jumping potential, and you will be able to control the speed and pace at which you approach fences.

- As well as using hacking to get your horse fit, use the opportunities it offers to improve your horse's balance and surefootedness: trot and canter up and down gradients when the going is suitable.
- Set up showjumps at home to imitate some of the types of fences you may meet in competition, such as arrowheads, V-fences and bounces. If your horse is very inexperienced, it can be a very safe way of introducing such obstacles.
- Look out for cross-country schooling days advertised locally, or hire a course to practise over so you can quietly introduce your horse to a variety of fences he may not have seen before which you cannot reproduce at home (such as water and ditches).

Walking a cross-country course

It is important to walk a cross-country course just as carefully as you would a showjumping course. The schedule will state times when the course is open for inspection. If you've never done a cross-country competition before, you may find it helpful to ask your instructor or an experienced friend to accompany you to offer advice on the best way to tackle each fence.

- A course plan should be on display - study this first before actually setting off to look at the fences.
- Don't just walk the course once - leave enough time to walk it twice so you are really familiar with the route you will be taking, as well as the obstacles. In this way, you will be able to focus on your riding during the class, rather than panicking about where the next jump is located.
- Concentrate on what you are doing instead of strolling round, gossiping.
- Take a notepad and pencil with you so that you can jot down a quick plan of the course along with the location of each of the fences. Make a few notes about each fence so that you can look through it again later on.
- Make sure you walk the right course, in the right order. Differently coloured number markers will indicate which fences are to be jumped in each class.
- Some fences may have easier or harder alternatives to jump: harder routes are usually shorter but will save time. Check both options to help you decide which one to take, and also so that if you need to change your riding plan, you are not taken by surprise. Remember that you must jump between the flags, keeping the red one on your right and the white on your left.

Walking a cross-country course

- If there is a water jump, wear wellington boots so that you can wade into it to check how deep it is and what the bottom is like.
- Pace out the distances between each element of a combination fence so you know how many strides your horse will take between each, and whether you will need to adjust his speed, impulsion and length of stride.
- Inspect simple-looking fences just as carefully as the more obviously tricky ones.
- As well as the fences themselves, check the ground on both the take off and landing sides and also the areas between each jump. Watch out for tussocky, poached, hard, undulating and sloping ground, which could all affect the line you decide to ride.
- Be aware of varying light conditions which may cause problems - bright glare coming off water on a sunny day for example, or where you will be jumping from light into shade.
- Look for the position of the start and finish.
- If possible walk round the course again on the day of the competition itself. This will refresh your memory, and allow you to check on any changes in the going.

Getting to a show

Getting to a show can cause it's own headaches unless you have planned everything out well ahead of time.

- Should it be fairly close and the route you have to take not too busy, you may decide to hack there. Leave enough time to walk most of the way, because if your horse arrives hot, tired and blowing he will not give his best performance.
- Give your horse a short rest before warming up for your first class.
- Persuade someone to drive over and meet you at the venue with any extra equipment you might need but cannot carry with you.
- If you're going to be hacking, wear protective clothing over your show outfit to keep yourself clean. Place a light exercise sheet over your horse's quarters, and put a stocking and tail bandage over his tail to keep him as spotless as possible.
- Transporting your horse in a horsebox or trailer will allow you to attend shows which are further away. In the case of more local shows it will also mean less time spent in getting to them, and therefore a later start. You'll be able to take changes of saddlery and more equipment than if hacking, and the vehicle will double-up as a changing room if required.
- If you are going to hire a horsebox and driver for the day, make your booking in plenty of time.
- If you wish to hire a self-drive trailer, first of all check that your towing vehicle is capable of pulling it safely when laden. Secondly, you should ensure that the driver's motor insurance covers them to tow a trailer.
- When hiring a trailer, it's best to arrange to collect it the day or evening before the show.
- If you own your own vehicle, make sure it is kept regularly maintained and serviced. Prepare it the day before the show to save time on the morning.

Getting to a show

- In case you get a puncture, check that there is a spare tyre for the trailer (which is inflated to the correct pressure) and a jack strong enough to lift it.
- Join a vehicle rescue organisation in case of a breakdown.
- If your horse has not travelled for some time, practice loading him a couple of times in the weeks preceding the show.
- If you know he is not very good at loading, or is inexperienced, obtain professional help in teaching him to load and travel calmly and safely.
- Choose travelling rugs for your horse according to weather conditions.
- Even if you aren't going to a show and are just practising loading, you must always dress your horse in protective clothing to help prevent injury.
- The night before, and again on the morning of the show, check local traffic reports to find out if any delays are expected. You can then either allow more time for your journey or plan an alternative route.
- Travelling is more tiring for your horse than you might realise. A journey of one hour is equivalent to an hour of exercise, so after arriving leave enough time for him to have a brief rest before warming up for your first class.
- Don't be tempted to drive fast if you are running late. It is dangerous and if your horse has a bad journey, it may cause him to be difficult to load in future.
- Having arrived safely, drive carefully across the showground to the parking area, both for the safety of others and to ensure you do not shake your horse up excessively on any bumpy, uneven terrain.

The day before the show

You'll find there is plenty to get done the day before a show, so don't make any plans to engage in other time-consuming activities!

- Give your horse some gentle exercise in the morning so you don't tire him. If possible, turn him out for a few hours afterwards to graze and relax.
- Get out any paperwork you will need to take with you, including show passes.
- If you have your own horsebox or trailer, put down bedding, check fluid levels, tyre pressures, and that there is sufficient fuel. If you do not use the vehicle on a daily basis, start and run the engine to ensure there are no problems.
- Clean all your saddlery
- Prepare your horse's travelling clothes.
- When you bring your horse in again, groom him thoroughly and bath him if necessary (and if the weather is warm enough).
- Wash the grooming kit after bathing.
- Clean out and tap stud holes, re-plugging them afterwards.
- Do any plaiting which can be done in advance.
- Pick, or buy a buttonhole such as a single cornflower or small, tight rosebud. Keep it fresh by wrapping the end of the stem in damp tissue with a piece of cling film over the top to prevent moisture seeping out. Then pop it in the fridge overnight.
- Fill a spare haynet and water container to take with you.
- Mix up the morning feed to save a little time in the morning. Cover it to avoid attracting vermin.
- Stable your horse overnight if he is likely to be difficult to catch in the morning, or if he needs to be clean for a showing class.

The night before

There's quite enough to do on the day of a show without having a last minute panic because your lucky pair of socks is still in the wash or you can't remember where you left the plaiting kit. You may have done everything you can think of on the yard during the day, but there are still a few final preparations to do in the evening to ensure you don't end up running behind schedule in the morning.

- Thread lots of plaiting needles - this can save a lot of time, especially if you find your fingers tend to go all shaky with pre-competition nerves. Gather together everything else you will need for plaiting, in readiness for the morning

- Lay out all your show clothes.

- Check that you have clear directions to the showground and work out how long it will take to travel there, allowing a little extra time for traffic on the way. If you're hiring the services of a professional horse transporter, ring to confirm your booking, the show venue, and the time you wish to be collected at.

- Make up a packed lunch to take with you. If you are planning to buy food at the show instead, read through the schedule to make sure there will be caterers.

- If your horse is stabled, visit him last thing to check him over, and to skep out his bed to ensure he stays as clean as possible.

- Use your checklists to make sure you haven't forgotten anything.

- Have a quick mental run through of any dressage tests or cross-country courses you will be attempting.

- Get an early night so you'll be alert and refreshed in the morning.

- Remember to set your alarm clock!

The morning of the show

Make sure you leave plenty of time on the morning of the show in which to get everything done. Rushing around will unsettle your horse and you will be more likely to forget something vital, or to make a poor job of getting your horse looking his very best. It's better to have too much time on your hands than not enough.

- Give your horse his feed early enough for him to have at least one hour in which to digest it before travelling.
- Leave him to eat in peace and quiet while you go and have your own breakfast. Even if you don't feel like much, try to eat something: you have a busy day ahead and need to keep your energy levels up.
- If you won't be returning to your house again, remember to take all your show clothes, paperwork, lunch and buttonhole with you when you go back to the yard.
- Muck out, so you don't have to face it later when you are tired.
- Groom your horse and wash off any stains which have appeared overnight.
- Scrub his feet thoroughly, both hoof walls and soles.
- Plait, or finish any plaiting up not done the day before.
- Load up all your equipment, using your checklists to make sure you have everything.
- Dress your horse for travelling, and load him up.

Arriving at the showground

Park up when you arrive at the showground. You may be told where to do this, but if not, choose somewhere reasonably secluded where you can get on with your last minute preparations without too many distractions from others.

- If you have a side ramp, it is a good idea to take a couple of plastic traffic cones with you which you can place by it to stop others from parking too close for you to use it.
- It's best not to leave any valuables unattended, but if you do have to, make sure they are placed out of sight and securely locked up. Remember to remove the keys from your vehicle's ignition.
- Don't unload your horse straight away, but leave him inside to settle for a few minutes whilst you go to the Secretary's tent.
- At the Secretary's tent, collect your numbers, make any late entries, and check whether classes are running on time. Sometimes you will have to pay a returnable deposit for numbers, so make sure you have enough money with you.
- If you have different numbers for each class you have entered, make a note on the back of them so you don't get confused and wear the wrong ones.
- On the way back to your horse, find out where all the rings are which you will be competing in. It's also good to know the location of collecting rings, practice fences and toilets.
- The general atmosphere and all the activity going on around the showground is exciting for some horses, so you may find it helpful to ride him quietly round in walk for half an hour before settling to serious work. This will give him the chance to get used to all the sights and sounds so he is relaxed and calm when you are ready to start working in for your class.

Nerves

It's perfectly normal to get nervous before a competition, but try not to allow it to reach the point where you can neither ride your best nor enjoy the day.

- Pre-class nerves can actually be an asset (as long as you can stop them from getting out of hand), putting an edge on your performance and stopping you from becoming complacent.

- Visualise yourself jumping clear, or receiving a rosette. Replace any negative thoughts you have with positive ones.

- Don't waste time worrying for days beforehand about things that might never happen: try to carry on as normal. But if you find you just can't do that, think of all the worst things that could occur and work out how to deal successfully with them. Then, go further and devise ways you could prevent them happening in the first place. If you have covered all eventualities, you should feel a little more confident and ready for anything.

- Bach Flower Rescue Remedy can be useful: you can also give it to your horse if you feel he gets as keyed up about things as you.

- Concentrate on your breathing for a few minutes to help relax yourself. Nervousness or concentrating hard can make you breathe shallowly and irregularly, leading to a lot of tension and stiffness which will make your riding less effective.

- The more you compete, the less worrying you will find it.

- Don't throw yourself in at the deep end. Enter small shows where you won't feel that everyone else is bound to be better than you.

- It's unlikely you will be the only one feeling nervous on the day!

Assistants

Although it is quite possible to cope on your own at a show, an extra pair of hands is always helpful. If you are new to competing, you may also find it reassuring to know there will be at least one familiar face at the show cheering you on from the sidelines.

- Remember to tell your assistant what time you'd like them to meet you if they're not travelling with you to the show.

- The day before the show, brief your helper as to what you want them to do. Have a quick rehearsal if there is anything they're not sure how to do.

- If you are taking part in a showing class, your assistant can come into the ring when it is time to 'strip off' your horse for the judge's inspection. He or she can help remove the saddle and place it behind the line up, brush off any saddle marks, then assist you in re-saddling and mounting again afterwards.

- Don't forget to make provision for some lunch for your helper. Pack some extra food or take along enough money to buy drinks and food from the show caterer.

- Tempers can become a little frayed when the pressure is on. Try not to snarl at your helper who is only trying to do their best, and may be feeling just as nervous about their responsibilities as you are about the competition. If you do get grumpy, be sure to apologise.

Keeping clean

Especially if taking part in a showing class, once you have got everything spotless, you will need to try and keep it that way if all your work is not to be wasted.

- If you can, keep your horse stabled the night before the show. Put down a big, deep clean bed so stable stains are kept to a minimum. In warm weather, putting a light summer sheet on will also help keep the coat clean, dust free and flat.

- On the morning of the show, place the tail inside one leg of a pair of tights and then bandage over the top to hold it in place. This will keep it clean whilst travelling, and can be left on until the last moment so the tail hairs don't become soiled.

- Protect velvet browbands by either wrapping a piece of cling film round them or buying a purpose-made browband cover.

- Pop a saddle cover over your saddle to keep it dust and dirt free whilst in transit. Bridles can be placed in a black dustbin liner.

- Pick up any droppings from inside the horsebox, trailer, or the area in which your horse is tied up outside so he doesn't stand in them.

- Don't allow your horse to nibble at grass or a haynet for half an hour before you tack up (or whilst tacked up) to avoid coloured saliva making his bit all dirty.

- Warm your horse up using a spare girth, and change it just before your class for a clean one. Remember to check that it is tight enough both before and after mounting.

- Even if you aren't going to use a numnah during the class, warm your horse up with one to keep the saddle lining clean.

- Wear a second-best pair of riding boots and put a track suit or shell suit over the top of your jodhpurs and shirt to keep them clean while warming up. Remove them and put on your jacket and smart boots just before your class.

Keeping clean

- Wear a pair of rubber washing up gloves whilst doing mucky jobs such as putting in studs, oiling feet or applying coat gloss. This will keep your hands clean and dirt free so you don't end up accidentally staining your clothing.
- Ask your assistant to hold your horse while you change into your show boots, and then mount directly from the lorry or trailer ramp. This will stop the soles of your boots getting dirty and messing up the stirrup irons and your horse's sides.
- Take a packet of disposable 'freshen up' wipes to use on your hands or face in case they become grimy during your last minute preparations.

Walking a showjumping course

Usually around ten or fifteen minutes before the start of your class, you will be allowed to walk round the course. It's important not to miss this opportunity as you can't always get a good view of all the fences from the ringside, and may not pick up on any potential problems caused by their siting. Walking round the course is the best way of learning it.

- Before you go in the ring, check the course plan. It is normally situated near to the ring entrance or pinned onto the declaration board. As well as showing a layout of the course, it will also tell you which fences will be used in the jump-off.

- After you have walked the course once, go round it a second or even a third time if necessary to really fix it in your mind.

- Don't amble round, or you may not have time to walk the course as many times as you would like.

- Walk the course taking exactly the same line on which you intend to ride your horse. This will give you a better feel for how much room you have to make turns in, and once mounted, will make it easier for you to remember the course.

- Decide whether you will get the best approach to the first fence from the left or the right rein. The positioning of the second fence in relation to it may also have a bearing on this.

- Always look ahead from the fence you are inspecting towards the next one so you can work out the best line to take.

- Watch out for 'traps' set by the course builder. For example, if a fence is jumped heading away from the collecting ring, you may need to ride your horse forwards more positively so he doesn't hang towards the other horses.

Walking a showjumping course

- Stride out any doubles and combinations so you can decide on the best strategy to take with your horse - whether to ask for fewer, longer strides, or to fit in more, but shorter ones. If you do not know how to do this, ask your instructor to show you.

- Look out for any difficulties which might be posed by the ground: for example, a slight slope or tussocky patches of grass.

- Make a note of where the start and finish boards or timing equipment is located, so you will remember to ride through them.

- If your instructor or a more experienced friend offers to walk round with you, listen carefully to their advice. Concentrate on what you are doing, and don't be distracted by others who want to chat.

- However simple a fence may appear, always inspect it properly.

- Once you have memorised the first round course, walk round the jump-off course too. This will be your only chance to do so, and will enable you to see where turns can safely be made tighter, and to plan the best timesaving route.

- Just before you leave the ring, look back at the fences again, and run through the course in your mind one more time.

- Leave the ring when a judge or ring steward asks you to clear the course.

- Once you have finished walking the course, put your number down on the declaration board, which is usually a blackboard near the ring entrance. You will jump in this order so don't put it too near the top. About halfway down will give you time before you need to get your horse ready to watch a few riders jump so you can see how well the course is riding, and whether any fences or turns are creating problems. It will also allow enough time for you and your horse to catch your breath again before a second or jump-off round.

Warming up

Classes can be won or lost whilst warming up in the collecting ring. This is the time when you should be concentrating on getting your horse supple and attentive, not allowing his attention to wander or overdoing things and exhausting him before his class. The warm up area is a place to prepare yourself and your horse mentally and physically, not to show off or school in. If he can't already do what you ask, now is not the time to try and teach him.

- Leave enough time before your class to warm up. Every horse varies as to how long they need. You will soon learn what is right for yours as you gain more experience at shows.

- Warm up areas can become busy places immediately before a class, so keep your wits about you. The same rules apply as when riding with others in a school. Pass left shoulder to left shoulder; the fastest gait has right of way; and lateral work has precedence over those in two-track work. Be aware of other horses around you and what they are doing.

- If asking your horse to slow down or halt, check that there is nobody immediately behind you before doing so.

- Two practice fences - a spread and an upright - are generally provided for jumping classes. They should be flagged as for competitions: make sure you approach them in the direction indicated, keeping the red flag on your right and white on the left.

- Start with something easy and inviting for your first practice fence, such as a small crosspole to help get you both going forward and feeling confident.

- Never approach or jump a practice fence if someone is adjusting it, or if cups are left on the wings without a pole resting on them.

Warming up

- Don't jump a practice fence which is higher than anything you will meet in the competition.

- If someone is hogging a practice fence or building it too high, ask them politely to allow you access or to lower it. Don't get into an argument if this doesn't work: ask the collecting ring steward to take action instead.

- Don't jump the practice fence more than you need to. Four or five times should be quite sufficient. Assuming that you are entering two classes - during which you will jump around twelve fences in the first round of each, followed by another six or eight in the jump-off - you could be jumping a total of between thirty six and forty fences. Add onto this the number of fences you jump in practice before each class and each jump-off, and it is easy to understand how overdoing practice can result in a very tired horse.

- If the collecting ring is very crowded and you are finding it hard to jump the practice fence safely, find out if there is a separate Clear Round class. You will then be able to go and pop around a few fences there instead, with the whole ring to yourself.

- If saddlery or clothing needs to be changed or removed, or you want to carry out any last minute finishing touches, try to do this ten minutes before you are due to go in the ring. You will then still have a few more minutes left before you are called, during which you can both work quietly so you are fully prepared.

- Keep your horse moving just before it is your turn to go, even if only in an active walk. If you allow him to stand around, you may lose his attention, or he may be inclined to nap to the other horses when you ask him to move on again. If you need to watch a few other competitors, do this earlier, before you start warming up.

Finishing touches

If you are competing in showing classes, a few last finishing touches just before you go in the ring will ensure that both you and your horse really look the part.

- Secure your number to your jacket either using thread of the same colour, or with nappy safety pins pushed through from the inside. Make sure it is the right way up and can be seen by the judge.
- Use a clothes brush or lint roller to remove any hairs and dust from your jacket.
- Tidy up any stray hairs escaping from plaits with a little hair gel. A dab of baby oil along the top will help make them shine.
- Apply a coat of hoof oil to the feet.
- Clean the eyes, nose and dock with separate damp sponges, then wipe the muzzle, around the eyes, and the dock with a little baby oil applied with a piece of cotton wool.
- Cover socks with chalk powder and brush off the excess to give a sparkling white finish.
- Prevent your horse from being irritated by flies by using a fly repellent. Use a fine spray from a pump action bottle. Don't use a cloth as it will mark the coat, making it look patchy.
- Whether you apply quartermarks or sharks teeth is largely a matter of personal preference, but do check beforehand to ensure they are appropriate for the class you are entering. They will not deceive a good judge if you hope they might conceal any weaknesses in conformation, and are more likely to draw attention to them. If they are to enhance your horse's appearance and not detract from it, they need to be neat and symmetrical when viewed from the rear, so practise doing them at home. This will also help you decide on what suits your horse best, and where and how much of a pattern to apply for maximum effect. The coat will need to be very clean and shiny, and neither will work on greys unless the coat is a very dark, iron colour.

Riding a dressage test

Although dressage tests don't actually begin until you enter the arena, you should still try to create a good initial impression in the judge's mind. Whilst waiting for the signal to start, ride around the edge of the arena on your horse's best rein, keeping him balanced and active.

- Don't panic the moment you hear the starting signal. Keep calm and stay focused on maintaining a nice rhythm and producing a straight entry down the centre line.
- Don't rush your horse through the test - it's not a race!
- No matter how brilliantly your horse goes, if he isn't accurate you won't get good marks. Ride corners and accurate transitions, begin and finish movements at the appropriate markers, and make sure that circles really are round in shape.
- Look upwards, not down at your horse. This will help you keep your position better, and if you are looking where you are going you will ride more precisely.
- When riding changes of rein across the diagonal, aim a little towards the inside of the markers rather than directly towards them. This will make it easier to prevent your horse from falling in on his shoulder, and to obtain a correct bend through the corner.
- If things go wrong, keep smiling, put the mistake behind you, and concentrate on riding the next movement.
- If halts aren't perfect, it is generally best not to fiddle with them and risk making matters worse.
- When making a turn down the centre line from inside the arena, it's preferable to undershoot rather than overshoot them.
- At the end of your test, establish your halt and salute by holding your reins (and whip if carried) in your left hand, dropping your right hand by your side and then nodding your head forward.

Riding a showjumping course

When it's your turn to go into the ring, remember to be positive. The moment you enter the ring, send your horse forward into trot and then canter so you are both thinking forward.

- Remember to wait for the bell or starting signal before beginning your round, or you will be eliminated. Take care not to cross through the start or finish line whilst you are waiting.
- Don't panic the moment you hear the bell and throw your horse at the first fence. If you aren't quite ready, ride another circle so you can approach the first fence well.
- Try to keep a good, regular and forward-going rhythm. Pushing on one moment and pulling back the next will distract your horse, put him off balance and undermine his confidence.
- Ride towards the centres of fences, approaching them straight and not at an angle.
- Don't look back if you hear a pole being rattled. You can't do anything about it, and it's more important to concentrate on what lies ahead.
- Always look ahead to the next fence, keeping your eye on it through every turn so you do not end up over- or undershooting your line.
- Ride as positively to the last fence as the first and remember to go through the finish line.

Jump-offs

Try to stay calm if you get into the jump-off so you don't make any silly mistakes. You should already know which fences will be used, so run through them in your mind, and the route you will take.

- Most jump-offs are ridden over a shorter but slightly higher course than the first round, and are timed, with the fastest clear round being declared the winner.
- You must ride in the order you are drawn in. Listen carefully to the public address system when it is announced so you know how much time you have to get ready. The numbers will also be put up on the declarations board.
- If you have a young or novice horse, it may be better to aim for a slow but clear round instead of trying to achieve a fast one, so you do not risk unbalancing or overexciting him.
- Don't gallop your horse on as fast as you can. Jumping at speed will make him more likely to knock down fences and your turns will be very wide, wasting more precious seconds than you gain.
- If you do need to need to cover long distances between fences more rapidly, rather than just hurrying, ask your horse to lengthen his stride so that he maintains balance and impulsion.
- If you have planned a tight turn after a fence, approach it on a short, bouncier stride so you can re-balance and manoeuvre quickly on landing.
- Take care not to turn so tightly that it causes your horse to slip or have insufficient time to see and weigh up the fence ahead.
- Don't risk jumping a fence at an angle.
- Keep your horse moving on after the last fence, as the clock will not stop until you have crossed the finish line.

Ringcraft

Having put a lot of time and effort into turning yourself and your horse out immaculately, you do not want to then let yourselves down because you fail to present yourselves well in the ring, or behave in an unmannerly fashion.

- Don't ride round and round in circles in front of the judge trying to catch his eye.

- Try to avoid getting too close to any horses that are being fractious.

- Don't get bunched up between other horses. If you need more space to allow your horse to move freely forwards, try going deeper into the corners to create some room between yourself and the horse in front. If necessary, ride a small circle and find yourself another gap to slot into, but do not overtake other competitors right in front of the judge. It is not a wise idea to overtake on the outside either as you could get trapped between other horses and the ring ropes.

- Keep a close eye on the ring steward, as they will pass on instructions from the judge as to what they want you to do next.

- Whilst riding round as a class, don't crowd the person in front. It may cause their horse to crab sideways, and you run the risk of yours getting kicked.

- Even if you think the judge is looking at another horse, ride as though he is are watching you: keep your horse balanced and attentive. Judges sometimes look back over their shoulders, and you don't want to get caught unawares.

- In some classes the judge may ride your horse. If this is the case, have your horse ready for him, girth tightened and with the stirrups adjusted to what you think is approximately the right length. Do not give him a long list of "dos and don'ts". If your horse is that difficult to ride, he probably shouldn't be in the class in the first place.

- Don't give up if you are initially put low down in the line-up. Continue to do your best as the situation can often change considerably after the individual inspection and show, or if the judge rides him.

- Don't sit sloppily, gossip with other competitors, or allow your horse to misbehave whilst standing in the line-up.

- When it is your turn to bring your horse out of line to be inspected by the judge, if he has been wearing a saddle, make sure it has been removed in readiness.

- Lead him straight out towards the judge, but not so close that they have to take a step back.

- If the judge asks you for any information about your horse, be polite and to the point - they won't want (or have the time to hear) an entire life history.

- Stand him up for the judge to assess the conformation, positioning yourself by the head so as not to block the view or get in the way. When asked to run him up, walk away, turn him smoothly away from you and then trot back towards and past the judge.

- When running up your horse in hand, look at a fixed point ahead of you so you both move in as straight a line as possible.

- During an 'in hand' class, you will usually all walk around in a clockwise direction. Lead from the near side so that the judge can see your horse clearly. Try to keep his head straight, rather than turned towards you, and if asked to trot remember to steady and balance him through the corners.

- Try to remain calm at all times.

- Never argue with the judge.

Riding a cross-country course

Riding round cross-country fences is an exhilarating experience, but be careful not to get carried away and throw all caution to the wind.

- If your horse has been plaited for an earlier phase of a one day event, remove the plaits so that you have a handful of mane to hold onto in an emergency.
- Use boots or bandages to protect your horse's legs.
- Make sure that your horse is sufficiently well-schooled to not get out of control but slow down and steady when you ask him to.
- Although you should already have decided on a riding plan, be prepared to adapt it a little if necessary. If your horse has problems at a particular fence, for example, choose easier options at successive obstacles until he's recovered his confidence.
- If your horse is struggling or becomes very tired, be self-disciplined enough to retire him from the class.
- Treat all the fences with respect: even the simplest may catch you both out if you approach it complacently.
- Approach fences which involve a change of level to lower ground on the far side (such as drops, steps and ski-jumps) from a shorter, bouncier stride.
- When tackling combinations, make sure you stay on your line for, and ride positively towards, the last element.
- Don't approach or try to ride fast through water, as the drag of it around your horse's legs could cause him to lose his balance and tip over. You will need to have plenty of impulsion though, especially if you will be jumping up out of it.
- Once you have passed the finish line, slow down gradually, then dismount and walk your horse until he has stopped blowing.

Safety

Safety around horses is as important at competitions as any other time, so don't neglect it in the heat of the moment. Bear in mind that shows are often attended by spectators who have little or no knowledge of the correct way to approach or behave around horses.

- Never attempt more than you or your horse can cope with.
- Ride sensibly, according to the weather conditions. If the ground is very hard, or becoming very churned up, it may be wiser to scratch from the competition rather than invite injury to yourself or your horse.
- Keep an eye out for any horses which become loose on the showground. Unless it is yours or you know it very well, keep away and allow the owner and show officials to deal with it.
- If another horse is being difficult or fractious, give it a wide berth, both for your own safety and to avoid making the situation worse.
- Never leave your horse unattended whilst tied up outside your vehicle. Always tie him to a piece of string, using a quick-release knot.
- Despite every possible precaution being taken, accidents can still happen. Although a well-run show should have made provision for this with a first aid organisation in attendance and a vet either present or on call, it is still a good idea to have a basic knowledge yourself of first aid procedures for both horses and humans.

Courtesy and manners

Being considerate and showing good manners will do a lot to make the day of a show more enjoyable for everybody. Do your best to set a good example!

- Be ready to go in the ring when your class or number is called. If for some reason you are late, apologise to the ring steward and ask if it is all right to go in.
- If the judge will ride your horse during a showing class, check that the girth is tight enough before they mount. Offer to give a leg up, or hold the offside stirrup leather whilst they are mounting to ensure that the saddle remains straight.
- If you know the person who is judging, don't be over familiar with them. Treat them as you would any other official so as to avoid causing embarrassment.
- Don't stand in the way of exits or entrances to rings. You will get in the way of other competitors trying to get in or out, and could end up getting kicked or causing their horse to nap.
- Keep your opinions to yourself. Unless you have something pleasant to say, don't gossip about others or openly criticise riders or their horses.
- Either take your rubbish home with you or dispose of it in the receptacles provided.

Courtesy and manners

- Be polite to show officials and judges, and never get into arguments.
- Show organisers and judges often put a lot of time and hard work into setting up and running shows for little or no recompense: try to spare a minute to thank them. If they feel that their efforts have been appreciated, and you have played your part in helping things to run smoothly, they are more likely to run another show in the future.
- Bad language is never acceptable.
- If you feel you have a genuine cause for complaint, or are unhappy about the way in which someone is behaving or treating their horse, go through official channels at the Secretary's tent.
- Only ride and work your horse in designated areas.
- Be considerate of spectators and other people on foot whilst you are mounted. Remember that small children may be less aware of the dangers which can be posed by horses.
- If you end up out of the line-up for ribbons in a showing class, it is bad manners to leave the ring before you are asked to.
- Be considerate to your horse too - he is not a mobile grandstand. Dismount between classes, loosen his girth or remove the saddle, and make him comfortable. Don't gallop around or keep working him just to show off in front of others.

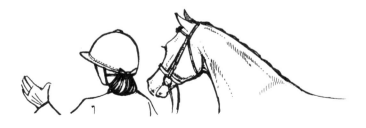

Competing in winter

Competing isn't an activity confined just to the warmer months of the year: you will find plenty of opportunities for showjumping and dressage during the winter at indoor venues too. If both you and your horse are to have fun and do well, you will need to be prepared to cope with weather conditions which are often less than ideal.

- Allow extra time for travelling, as bad weather can cause delays.
- During freezing weather watch out for dangerous icy patches when loading or unloading your horse, and also when walking him from the parking bay to the warm up area.
- If hacking to the show, arrange for someone to meet you there with a rug for your horse and a snug jacket for you. Although you may be nicely warm by the time you arrive, if neither of you has much to wear, you will both quickly become chilled if there is much waiting around between classes.
- Although the competition may be held indoors, the warm up area will not necessarily be under cover. Keep an eye out for boggy patches and, if jumping, for deep, churned up approaches and landings forming at practice fences.
- Take a thermos filled with a hot drink to warm you up on the inside.

Competing in winter

- Remember waterproofs for you and your horse in case it rains. Being wet increases the chill factor and makes you feel colder.
- Wear gloves, as they will not only keep your fingers warm, but give you a better grip on your reins if they become wet and slippery.
- Use leg protectors on your horse when transporting him rather than bandages. They will be much easier and quicker to take off and put on in cold weather when he may not feel like standing still for long and your fingers may not be as nimble.
- If you're feeling chilly, a hand warmer really will help you feel better. Small 'single use' disposable packs or rechargeable sachets are ideal since they are safe and easy to use and slim enough to slip into a jacket pocket without creating an unsightly bulge.
- A pair of chaps will do a lot to help keep you warm, dry and clean when warming your horse up before a class, and are quick and easy to put on or take off. Thermal underwear and socks are also a good investment.
- Remember to allow more time for warming your horse up before a class in cold weather.
- In really bad weather, ring the show secretary before leaving to check that the show is still on.

Competing indoors

Shows are held throughout the year at both outdoor and indoor venues. Both have their various pros and cons. Whilst it is pleasant to be outdoors during fine weather, covered arenas do mean that even during the winter, competitions can still be run.

- Indoor venues have a major advantage in that provided it has been properly maintained, the going is always good. Watch out for those surfaces which have not been so well cared for though - one which is packed hard beneath a shallow layer of loose top material can make for treacherous footing.

- Keep an eye out too for any slightly boggy areas created by poor or leaky sprinkler systems.

- Space tends to be more limited when indoors, so if show jumping, walk the course very carefully, planning how to make the best use of what's available.

- You will need to know the course very well, since the fences will all be placed much closer together than outdoors. Everything will seem to happen much more quickly and there won't be time to look for the next jump if you start to lose your way.

- If your horse has never been in a covered arena before, he may be a little anxious at first. Prepare him in advance of the show by taking him for a lesson or schooling session at an indoor school belonging to a local riding centre or livery yard.

- When the lights are on, shadows being cast may worry your horse or create false ground lines in front of fences.

- The public address system or the noise of spectators clapping or cheering may sound much louder indoors than when outside, which some horses can find a little alarming.

Competing in hot weather

Hot weather can produce its own particular problems for competitors. Apart from the dangers of over exertion in such conditions, during long dry spells of weather the ground is often very hard, which can be punishing on the legs of your horse. Rather than risk his soundness, it may be wise to consider entering fewer classes, or even to withdraw from them.

Vehicle interiors can become very hot, so find somewhere shady outside for yourself and your horse to stand between classes.

Wear light coloured, loose fitting cotton clothing.

If taking your own lunch, pack it in an insulated cooler box or bag. Sip fluids regularly to ensure that you don't become dehydrated. Isotonic sports drinks are ideal.

Wiping your face, hands and round the back of your neck with a damp sponge will make you feel refreshed.

Apply sunscreen to exposed areas of your skin and, if your horse has a pink muzzle susceptible to sunburn, put some sunscreen on it too. Do not use baby oil as part of your finishing touches.

Encourage your horse to drink regularly too. On finishing a class, offer him water and allow him to take a few swallows every ten to fifteen minutes until he has cooled down.

If your horse is reluctant to drink when at competitions, try holding the bucket for him. Take along a wet haynet for him to pick at also, to increase his water intake.

Take along a large container of water so you can wash him down after a class to help cool him off. Use plenty of water, and alternate washing with short periods of walking.

Overweight horses are at greater risk of overheating because body fat is a good insulator and stops them cooling down as quickly.

First aid

It is a good idea to buy or make-up travelling first aid kits for bot[h]
humans and equines - kept in separate boxes - which you can take t[o]
shows with you. A knowledge of basic first aid for both [is]
invaluable, enabling you to deal with any minor problems which ma[y]
occur or to take the appropriate action whilst waiting fo[r]
professional veterinary or medical assistance to arrive. A suggeste[d]
list of items for you to include are:

Human first aid kit

- Sticking plasters
- Headache tablets
- 2 x crepe bandages
- Triangular bandage
- Non-adhesive
  sterile dressings
- Cotton wool
- Sachets of sterile water
- Antiseptic cream
- Tweezers
- Scissors
- Small plastic bowl
- Sterile eye solution
- Eye bath
- Insect after-bite treatment

Horse first aid kit

- Large roll of cotton wool
- Roll of gamgee
- 4 x crepe bandages
- 4 x stable bandages
- Scissors
- Large non-adhesive
  sterile dressings
- Roll of surgical gauze
- Antiseptic spray
- Thermometer
- Sachets of sterile water
- Self-adhesive bandage
- Small plastic bowl
- Vet's telephone number

At the end of the day

Win or lose, when you get home remember to put your horse first. There'll be plenty of time to relive the highs and lows of the competition with your friends and family later.

- On arriving home, make your horse comfortable: remove any plaits, and brush off sweat marks.
- Check him over carefully for any injuries you may not have noticed earlier.
- If possible, and it's warm enough, turn him out in the field for a few hours to graze and relax.
- If your horse will be having a rest day following the show, reduce the size of his evening feed to take account of this.
- Visit him later in the evening to ensure he isn't suffering any undue effects after the exertions of the day.
- Unload all your saddlery and equipment from the horsebox or trailer and put it away safely. Muck out the vehicle too, so the floor can dry.
- The next day, let your horse take it easy. Turn him out to graze or take him out for a gentle hack to help ease any stiffness.
- If he seems to have taken a lot out of himself, ask yourself why so you can make sure he doesn't overdo things next time. It could be that you entered too many classes, or that he wasn't fit enough.
- Clean all your saddlery thoroughly.
- Wash your own and your horse's show clothes, and store them away neatly, ready for next time.
- While it's still fresh in your mind, add to your checklists any extra items that you forgot to take this time.
- Make a note of things you are getting low on and will need to get hold of before the next show - such as coat gloss or plaiting thread.

Improving performance

Once the show is over and your horse has been made comfortabl
for the night, you will have time to reflect on how things went durin
the day. Whether you had a successful outing or not, you will fin
there is always room for further improvement.

- Look out for schooling days and clinics being held locally. Even i
  you cannot get a place to ride on one, you can still learn a lot b
  going along to watch.
- Go to some of the bigger horse shows to watch some of the to
  riders in action. As well as learning, you will often find it helps t
  inspire you and renew any flagging enthusiasm.
- Keep a competition notebook. Make entries in it after each show
  jotting down any comments made by judges or handy tips yo
  discover which will help you to do even better in the future. Writ
  down anything you feel you did wrong too, so you don't forge
  and repeat the same mistakes. You can also make notes about th
  show generally, such as the standard of entries, ring sizes, parkin
  and other facilities, so that if you find any competition date
  clashing the following year it will help you decide which one you'
  prefer to attend.
- Read and keep for future reference any useful features o
  schooling and competing which you find in horsy magazines.
- Many professional riders and trainers run occasional workshop
  and lecture-demonstrations which are well worth attending t
  further your knowledge and pick up further 'tricks of the trade'
  Some may also have produced videos which you can buy or ren
  to watch at home.

Improving performance

- Remember to collect your score sheets at the end of a dressage test. Read through all the comments carefully, and work at improving weak areas during schooling sessions.
- If you feel that either your own or your horse's confidence suffered a bit of a setback during the competition, spend some time quietly schooling at home to remedy the matter, returning to earlier stages of work if necessary. When you are ready to compete again, enter a few easier and smaller classes to begin with: for the sake of experience, you can always ask to take part 'Hors Concours' should your current winnings restrict you from entering competitively.
- Ask someone to use a camcorder to video you whilst riding at shows. In addition to being a nice record to have, it can be useful in analysing when and why any problems occurred.
- If you experienced real difficulties, have lessons with a good instructor who will also be able to accompany you on your next outing to give on-the-spot advice and assistance.
- At the end of a showing class, ask the judge for advice on how to improve your placing the next time out.
- Find out if there are any competition/schooling days being held locally. These involve receiving 20 - 30 minutes of individual instruction on riding through a dressage test or round a course of jumps, followed immediately after by doing it for real, as a competition. This can be an invaluable way of overcoming nerves, and in improving specific aspects of performance; there is usually also a further opportunity to discuss it later with the judge and instructor.

Winning isn't everything

If you have been successful in your class, accept compliments and congratulations gracefully and enjoy the moment, but don't let it go to your head or make you become complacent in the future. In particular, beware of bragging or running down your fellow competitors!

- If you won or were placed in your class, you will usually be asked to go back into the ring to receive your rosette. Make sure you still look reasonably smart, and if you do a victory lap, don't gallop madly round, overtake or race other competitors.

- If you were placed lower than you hoped, don't become disheartened, or blame others. Keep learning and working hard and gradually you will start to find your results improving.

- Don't set unrealistic goals for yourself or your horse or you are bound to be disappointed.

- If you felt your horse didn't go as well as he could have, don't take him off and start schooling or jumping him.

- Win or lose, competing should be about having fun. Take the time to enjoy your horse, the company you find yourself in, and the day itself.

- It's not the end of the world if you don't win. Life goes on, and there will always be another show and another day.

Index

Index